Making the Modern World
Europe

East Europe

John Robottom

Longman

Murder in parliament

Yugoslavia is a federal country made up of six nations

Members of the IMRO (Independent Macedonian Revolutionary Organisation)

20 June 1928. A short, hot-tempered man was speaking in Parliament in Belgrade, the capital of Yugoslavia. Opposite, the Croat Peasant Party shouted and called out 'brigand! scoundrel!' This was too much. He drew a revolver. Five shots rang out. Stephen Raditch, the leader of the Croat Peasant Party, was taken to hospital to die.

Next day there were riots in Zagreb, the largest town in the part of Yugoslavia called Croatia. Men and women carried Croat flags wrapped in black; angry chants of 'Bloody Belgrade' were heard. But in Belgrade, which was in Serbia, many Serbs rejoiced. Raditch, like the rest of the Croats, was to them a loud-mouthed troublemaker.

An officer and the driver grapple with Georgiev who has just shot the King of Yugoslavia and the French Foreign Minister

Bitterness between Serbs and Croats went back to 1918. Before then there had been no Yugoslavia. Serbia was a small free kingdom. Slovenia, Bosnia and Croatia were ruled by Austria until she was beaten in World War One. Then the leaders of these people signed an agreement to join with Serbia. They all belonged to the race we call Slavs and so Yugoslavia—land of the southern Slavs—was born.

Most Serbs wanted to make Yugoslavia into 'greater Serbia'. The King, most of the government and nearly all the generals were Serbs. These leaders saw that Serbs got nearly all government jobs in the post office, tax office and police force.

They treated the people of south Serbia even worse than the Croats. South Serbia was really Macedonia but the Serbs had conquered it. No-one who spoke the Macedonian language was allowed to teach in a Macedonian school; the people had to speak Serbian. Macedonian farmers were cheated out of fair prices for their tobacco crop and many people starved.

After the murder of Raditch the King closed parliament and said he was going to be a dictator to force the Serbs and the other people to live peacefully. But some Croats joined a gang called the Ustasha. The Ustasha leader visited the chief of IMRO, a secret society which wanted to free Macedonia from Serbia. Shortly after, an IMRO thug, Georgiev, made his way to a secret camp where Ustasha terrorists were trained to use bombs and pistols.

In 1934 the King visited France. He landed at Marseilles and drove away in an open car. Suddenly, Georgiev dodged through the crowd, jumped on to the running board and fired twice. He was cut down by an officer's sword, but too late. The King of Yugoslavia was dying.

3

Eastern Europe between the wars

The map shows the countries of eastern Europe. Until World War One, or just before, all of them had been part of one of the empires of Germany, Austria, Russia or Turkey. So in 1919 they were all new states with great problems.

Unluckily in every one there were large numbers with a different language or religion from the rest of the nation. For example, in Poland there were eighteen million Poles but also five million Ukrainians, a million Germans and three million Jews. So each country suffered, like Yugoslavia, from quarrels between the nations which led to riots and murder.

All these lands, too, were poor. Two out of three of the people were peasants. Most of them had farms no bigger than two football pitches to feed a large family. Times were hard in the 1930s because farmers could get only very low prices for their crops.

The difficulties of making people live peacefully and finding work and food

The countries of eastern Europe between the wars

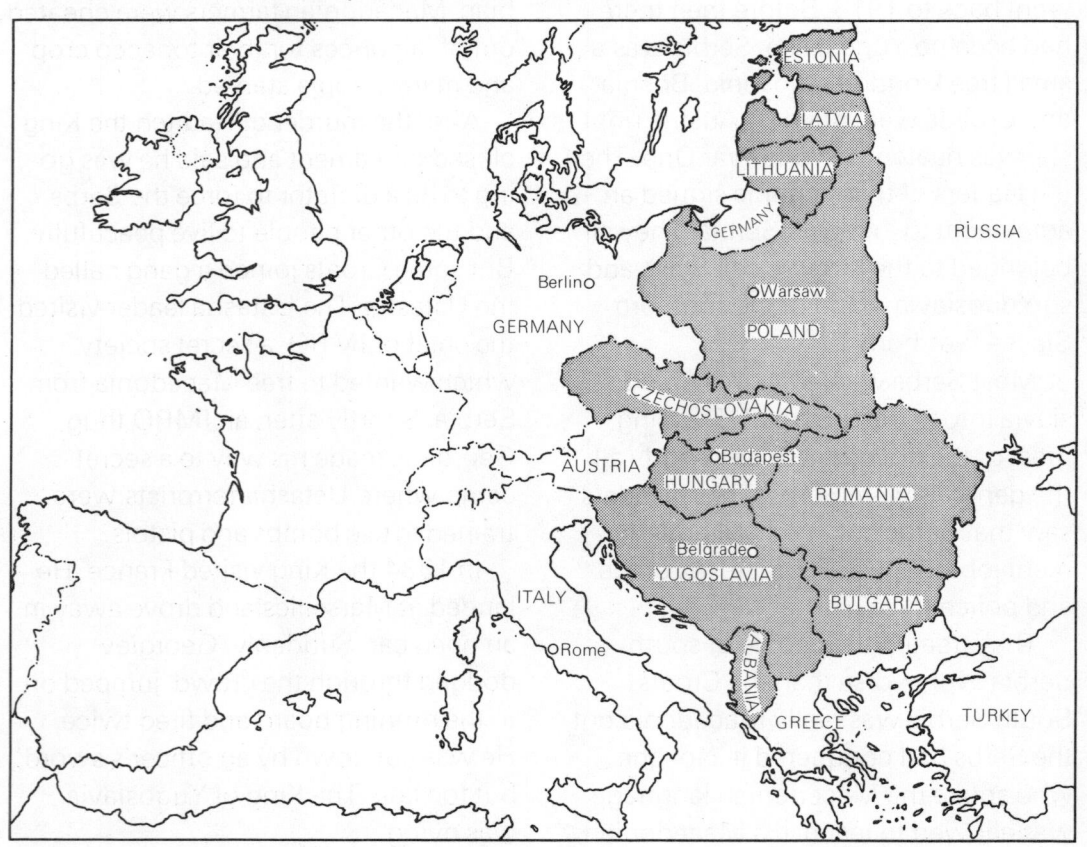

for everyone were too great for the first governments. One by one, dictators took over in all these countries except Czechoslovakia. Sometimes the dictator was a king; at others he was a soldier like Marshall Pilsudski in Poland.

Adolf Hitler was pleased at the weakness of eastern Europe. It made his drive to the east so much easier. He began by taking half of Czechoslovakia in 1938. In March 1939 he took the rest. In September 1939 his armies marched into Poland. Britain and France then declared war.

But they could do nothing to stop Hitler at first so the leaders of eastern Europe rushed to sign agreements promising not to fight Germany. This way they hoped she would not invade their countries. By 1941 only Yugoslavia stood aside. But she, too, expected invasion so her Prime Minister flew to sign a treaty with Hitler.

He returned to find that the people would not accept the deal. A group of army officers took over the government and got ready to stand up to Hitler. 'Yugoslavia', said Winston Churchill,' has found her soul.'

Hitler was furious. He ordered an invasion. Germans entered from the east and Italians from the west. In two weeks Yugoslavia was beaten and divided. Serbia was occupied by Germans. The Italians took over the coastal areas. In Croatia, the Germans gave power to the thugs who had murdered the King—the Ustasha.

Troops who fought with Marshall Pilsudski in World War One fight again—this time to make their leader dictator of Poland

German soldiers in 1941 occupy Sarajevo, the Yugoslav town where the heir to the Austrian throne had been murdered in 1914

Comrade Tito and the Comintern

Joseph Broz was born in Croatia in 1892. His father expected him to help in the fields and in his blacksmith's shop. But Joseph did not want to live always as a poor struggling peasant. He left home at fourteen and became a locksmith. Yet times were hard and often he could not find work.

In 1914 war broke out and Broz joined the army. He was captured and taken prisoner to Russia. This was the time of the Russian Revolution and Broz supported the Communists, the party of working men like himself.

He returned to find Croatia was part of Yugoslavia, and became one of the first members of the Yugoslav Communist Party. It was a strong party with much support from workers, whose pay and working conditions were terrible. But the government feared the spread of Communism and banned the Party in 1922. Only a few tough members remained.

Broz was one. He lived under false names trying to keep the Party alive as an underground organisation. In 1928 he was arrested and sent to prison for five years after being beaten up by the police.

His brave work was noticed. After he left prison he was called to work for the Comintern in Moscow. The Comintern, or Communist International, had been set up by the Russians as a headquarters for Communist Parties in every country of the world. The Russian ruler, Joseph Stalin, kept a tight grip on it and Comintern workers ran the risk of prison or death if they disagreed with him.

In Moscow, Broz could see that Stalin's rule was cruel and living conditions were terrible. But he had been there twenty years before, when things were even worse, so he would not

This passport contains 32 pages.
Ce passeport contient 32 pages.

PASSPORT
PASSEPORT
CANADA

No. of passport
No du passeport ⟩ 32829

Name of bearer
Nom du porteur ⟩ Spiridon Mekas

CANADA

Accompanied by his wife
Accompagné de sa femme ⟩

and............children
et de............enfants

NATIONAL STATUS Naturalized British
NATIONALITÉ Subject 25th July 1923 of Yugoslavian origin

Detta pass gäller för resa till:

Pays pour lese
port est va

utlandet, med undantag
av Spanien, de spanska
besittningarna och den
spanska zonen i Marocko.

l'étranger,
d'Espagne
egpagnoles e
espagnole au

Foto

to

Countries for which this passport is valid:

Dieser Pass
Reise nach

sinnehavarens egenhändiga namnteckning. Signature du
porteur. Signature of bearer. Unterschrift
des Passinhabers.

foreign countries, except
Spain, the Spanish colo-
nies and the Spanish zone
of Morocco.

dem Auslan
nahme Sp
spanischen
der spanisch
Marokko.

John A Carlsan

struns egenhändiga namnteckning. Signature de la femme.
Signature of the wife. Unterschrift der Frau.

Detta pass är gällande till den:
Ce passeport expire le:
This passport expires:
Dieser Pass ist gültig bis zum:

Two false passports used by Joseph Broz—or Tito—when he worked for the Comintern

criticise. He believed that a better future for working men everywhere could come only through communism, and communism could not spread without Russian help.

He was just the man Stalin wanted to take over as leader of the Yugoslav Communist Party. In 1938 he chose the last of his false names—Tito—and came home to rid the Yugoslav Party of men and women who Stalin thought were weak or unfaithful. Then he brought in new leaders and built up the number of members. In 1941 the Yugoslav Communist Party was stronger than ever before. But then the Germans came.

The partisans

Tito (centre) with two Partisan leaders during the war

'The hour has struck to take arms against the Fascist aggressors. Do your part in the fight for freedom under the leadership of the Communist Party.'

This message was printed secretly in Tito's flat in Belgrade and smuggled to every part of Yugoslavia in June 1941. The Germans had just attacked Russia and the communists wanted to help their comrades there. But even more they wanted to put themselves at the head of the Yugoslav resistance to the invaders.

Throughout the country men and women from the villages, led by communists, formed partisan bands. They armed themselves by killing German soldiers and taking their weapons. The Germans took a terrible revenge, executing ten Yugoslavs for every dead German. It was going to be a grim war but this did not stop the partisans. They fought on until they had cleared the Germans out of the mountains in western Yugoslavia. They called this the Liberated Area. Tito left Belgrade in dis-

Partisans crossing a mountain in western Yugoslavia

guise and joined them there.

When the partisans entered a village they destroyed the police station and all the police records. Then they burned tax records and lists showing who owned land. Most of the police and government officials fled or were killed. With every sign of the old government destroyed, the communists could begin building a new way of life.

They got the villagers to elect a People's Committee to run their affairs. Most of the men and women on the

People's Committee were communists. They got teams of men to build bridges, sink wells and repair war damage. Some villages had their first schools when an old building was turned into a schoolhouse.

In 1943 all the People's Committees sent a representative to a meeting of the Anti-Fascist Council, which elected a Committee to become the government of Yugoslavia when it was freed. Nearly all the new men were communists. Tito was named as Prime Minister.

Victory for Tito

But Yugoslavia was not free yet. The Liberated Area was under constant German attack. The partisans had to make long marches to escape them. The marches were led by young partisan soldiers in tattered uniforms carrying guns captured from the enemy. Then came a few captured trucks carrying supplies and the badly wounded. Alongside walked the less badly wounded. They could not be left behind because this was a cruel war in which both sides shot prisoners. At the rear followed thousands of old men, women and children who came because they knew their homes would be destroyed by the Germans or the Chetniks.

The Chetniks were an underground army formed to fight for the return of the old government and the king. At first they had fought the Germans but then they began to help them against the partisans. They would rather fight their own countrymen than see Yugoslavia become communist after the war.

The old Yugoslav government had flown to Britain and asked the British to help the Chetniks. So for two years the R.A.F. had dropped supplies and

Chetniks

Belgrade in October 1944 when the Germans were driven out

arms to the Chetniks. At this time no-one in England knew about the partisans. Then Churchill read reports that said that it was only the partisans who were killing Germans. He sent a British officer in, by parachute, to find out about Tito.

Brigadier Maclean reported back that Tito and the partisans were fighting the Germans and that the Chetniks were not. He told Churchill that Britain should give Tito as much help as possible but warned him that this would mean that Yugoslavia became communist after the war.

Churchill asked, 'Do you intend to make Yugoslavia your home after the war?' 'No', Maclean replied.

'Neither do I,' Churchill said. 'And that being so the less you and I worry about the form of government they set up the better . . . What interests us is, which of them is doing most harm to the Germans?'

In 1944 the British sent over 10,000 rifles, 50,000 sub-machine guns, 700 wireless sets and 260,000 pairs of boots to the Partisans. The Russians gave even more help.

For the first time the partisans were strong enough to begin full-scale action in the open country. They attacked at the end of 1944. At the same time the Russian army entered Yugoslavia. The Red Army and the partisans fought their way to Belgrade. On 20 October 1944 the Germans left the capital of Yugoslavia to Tito and the partisans.

Communist Yugoslavia

Tito now set about turning his country into a copy of Stalin's Russia.

First, Yugoslavia had to become a one-party state. The communists made up the largest part of the People's Front which was the only party allowed to stand for parliament. Only communists could make radio broadcasts; newspapers were closed unless they supported the People's Front. When nine out of ten Yugoslavs voted for the People's Front in 1945 Tito said, 'We knew how it would all end.'

Like the Russians he had a secret police. OZNA put thousands of enemies of the communists into prison or concentration camps. They were often brutal and many times arrested the wrong people but Tito backed them up: 'If OZNA puts fear into the heart of all those who do not like our kind of Yugoslavia, all the better for the Yugoslav people.'

The lands of the Roman Catholic Church were taken away and its schools were closed. Its Archbishop was sent to prison for sixteen years. Tito and the communists were atheists, who did not believe in God. They also knew the Church would try to stop the spread of communism.

Communism meant that no-one should have so much money that he could make others work for him. Private factory owners had decided what goods to make according to what gave the biggest profit; under communism the

Archbishop Stepiniac, head of the Yugoslav Catholic Church, on trial

12

government would decide for the good of the whole country. All farms and businesses were nationalised. Their work had to follow the Five Year Plan of 1946 which was meant to end Yugoslavia's terrible poverty. After five years she was to make ten times as much iron and have new factories for machine tools, electrical equipment and heavy machinery.

The Five Year Plan would give work in the factories to many peasants. But could the others grow enough food to feed all the people in towns? The answer to this problem was collective farms. Peasants had to give up their tiny plots to make a huge collective farm big enough to afford tractors and machinery. They would work in teams doing specialised jobs, almost like factory workers. This was the way Stalin said he had improved farming in Russia.

Roadbuilding was an important part of the Five Year Plan. Here soldiers are building the 'Unity of Brotherhood Highway' which linked Zagreb, the centre of Croatia, and Belgrade, the centre of Serbia

Russian satellites

Eastern Europe today

All the countries on this map followed Yugoslavia on the road to communism after the war.

People in the west called them 'satellites'. A satellite is a small star which follows a larger planet or star through the heavens. The countries of Eastern Europe were satellites of Russia. Most of their leaders had lived in Russia before the war working for the Comintern and waiting for a chance to return home. The chance had been the Second World War, for the Red army had marched through all Eastern Europe on their way to Berlin. After the Red soldiers, Russian planes flew in the communist leaders who were given important posts in the government.

Bulgarian co-operative farmers on holiday at a state health resort built for them

Industrial crops are important. These reeds will be used for extracting cellulose. A photograph taken in Roumania in 1959

In the next two or three years they set up one-party states and destroyed everyone who stood in their way. At every stage they had taken their orders from Stalin in Moscow. This take-over was possible because of the occupying Red Armies. There were about three million Russian soldiers in east Europe after the war. The cost of this huge army was paid by taxing the people in these terribly poor countries.

Stalin held eastern Europe in a tight grip because he was afraid of Germany. The war had followed from the easy way Hitler had been able to attack one after another of the countries of eastern Europe. Now Stalin kept eastern Germany and the other nations under close Russian control behind the 'iron curtain'. Their communist governments supported him in all his quarrels with America during the Cold War.

Stalin forced the satellites to help in the rebuilding of Russia. Each country made trading agreements which gave the Russians just the goods they wanted even if they were needed by eastern Europe. The Russians paid their own price too. Poland sold coal to Russia at a tenth of the price she could have got from Denmark.

There were tens of thousands of Russian 'advisers' in eastern Europe. Russian generals made the eastern European armies fit in with the plans of the Red Army. Russian managers ran the railways, airlines and shipping companies. All the time they were making profits for Russia—and the people of eastern Europe were paying.

Tito against Stalin

The Yugoslav Communist Party paper 'Struggle' told the people about the quarrel with the Russians. The bottom left headline reads 'Statement of the Cominform on the state of the Yugoslav Communist Party' and the bottom right, 'Our working people stand firm with the Central Committee and Comrade Tito'

In every other eastern European country the Red Army had fought the main battles against the Germans. In Yugoslavia they only helped the partisans in the last stages. They got few thanks. The Yugoslavs complained about Red soldiers who robbed or attacked women. Tito made Stalin angry by saying that both America and Russia were unhelpful to Yugoslavia.

Tito objected when the Russians did not pay their share towards the joint Yugoslav-Russian shipping companies and when they began to run Yugoslav airfields. He found that Yugoslavia could buy the British film 'Hamlet' for 2,000 dollars but paid Russia 20,000 dollars for 'The Exploits of a Soviet Intelligence Agent'. After two years he refused to allow Russia any share in Yugoslav business.

Stalin became angry, especially when he heard of Tito's visits to other east European countries. Crowds turned out to shout: 'Long Live Tito'. They admired Tito because he had led his people against the Germans and because he stood up to Russia. As Tito himself said, 'The Yugoslav brand of communism . . . was not imported ready-made from Moscow.' The last straw was Tito's suggestion that east

European countries should join together in a common market. This would have meant doing without Russian help. 'I will shake my little finger and there will be no more Tito', Stalin said.

He wrote to Tito accusing him of being a bad communist. Stalin believed that if the other Yugoslav leaders thought Tito was a bad communist they would choose a new leader who would follow Russia without question. But the leading Yugoslav communists trusted 'The Old Man' as they called Tito. They arrested the only Yugoslav supporter of Russia and sent a firm reply to Stalin.

His next move was to expel Yugoslavia from the Cominform, an organisation of communist parties set up to help Russia keep control of east Europe. He hoped this would turn the people against Tito. Tito called a meeting of the Yugoslav Communist Party. Two thousand members were chosen at meetings of the half million communists in Yugoslavia. Nearly every one had been a partisan. Tito spoke for eight hours. He reminded them of the hardships they had shared in the war and all they had done since to build a new Yugoslavia. At the end they elected him and all his close friends as their leaders again. Stalin had failed.

The quarrel with Russia did not stop work under the Five Year Plan. Men and women work in 1949 to build New Belgrade, today a modern city on the other side of the river from old Belgrade

Titoism

In 1948 Yugoslavia completely broke her friendship with Russia. But Tito still held that communism was the only answer to the problems that had troubled Yugoslavia before the war. He set out to build a communist country where communists were not kept in power by the secret police or the Red Army.

The most important word in Titoism is 'self-management'. Yugoslav factories are managed by their work people. They elect a 'workers' council' which sets up committees to look after different sides of the business. Most of the factory's earnings go to pay taxes; the rest is used to provide houses, clinics and so on for the workers. Communists usually make up the greatest number on a Workers' Council but they have to work hard for their position and can be turned out at elections.

Each of the different nations now has its own government. These six national Republics are nearly as important as the federal government headed by Tito. Today Macedonians, Croats, Bosnians are equal with the Serbs.

The peasants were allowed to leave co-operatives and farm their own land, provided no one farmer had more than forty acres. Farming is still poor but the living conditions of the peasants are getting better especially as new industries give work to those who would otherwise go idle and hungry in their villages.

Many east European communists supported Titoism. But not for long. Titoism became a crime for which leading communists were executed — on Stalin's orders. His grip on the rest of east Europe grew stronger.

Macedonia Today. Tito's government has done a great deal to make up for the illtreatment of the Macedonians before the war. This is Skopje, the capital of Macedonia.

Macedonia today. Peasants still wear traditional costume but their village may have electric light and the young boy will have learned to read and write

But Stalin died in 1953. Almost immediately there were anti-communist riots in East Germany. The new rulers of Russia saw that something must be done to make them more popular with the satellites. In 1956 Mr. Khrushchev made his 'secret speech' telling the Russian Communist Party just how wicked and cruel Stalin had been. Then he sacked Molotov, who had been Stalin's right-hand man in the attacks on Yugoslavia. After that he invited Tito to Russia.

Here Tito got Khrushchev to sign a document saying that there were many roads to communism and no way was better than another. If Khrushchev said this to Yugoslavia, must he not also say it to other east European countries? Tito thought so. On the way home he stopped in Roumania and made a speech in which he said: 'There are no more satellites.' Was he right?

Before Tito went to Moscow, Mr. Krushchev visited Yugoslavia and apologised for the quarrel of 1948

Poland

Crowds gather in Poznan at the beginning of the riot

The people of Poland had suffered under their Communist government. Even the Russians admitted they had robbed Poland of about £200 million by making them sell coal and other goods at very low prices. Collective farms had failed; there were only half as many animals per collective as there were on private farms. The Polish army was under the orders of a Russian officer.

In 1956 engineering workers in Poznan went on strike. The government would do nothing to improve their pay and conditions. So the strike became a riot. The rioters called for an end to Russian occupation and their pup-pet government. The Party leaders were so worried that they called Mr Gomulka back into the government. Gomulka was a popular communist who had been dismissed by Stalin for Titoism.

Russian leaders immediately flew to Warsaw to tell the Poles to dismiss Gomulka again. But the Poles stood up to them. Gomulka was left to carry on.

He began by clearing the old Stalinist gang out of the Polish Communist Party. The Russian general was sent home. Then Mr Gomulka set about taking Poland along a 'New Course'. He was firm about keeping her communist but, like Tito, he wanted to give

Mr Gomulka speaking in Warsaw in 1968

the people a greater share in the government. Two other parties were allowed
to stand for parliament and the elections
were fair enough to let some of their
candidates be elected. He freed the
head of the Roman Catholic Church
but would not let the Catholics open
schools again. The peasants were allowed to leave the collective farms.

Gomulka stayed in power in Poland
until December 1970. The country is
communist and people are not as free
as they are in some western countries.
But they are a lot freer than the Russians
and the U.S.S.R. have allowed Poland
to carry on with the New Course. Both
countries are agreed that they must
stay good friends. This is because of
Germany. If Germany ever again
became a war-like power the Poles
would suffer first and then the
Russians—as in World War Two. The
answer, say the Poles and Russians, is
firstly a united Eastern Europe with
their armies joined with the Russians in
the arrangement called the Warsaw
Pact. Secondly a smaller Germany; that
means that Poland should keep the
parts of Germany she was given at the
end of World War Two. Thirdly a divided Germany; which means East Germany must stay in communist hands.

Hungary

October 1956. Crowds of students, actors and writers march into Petofi Square in Budapest, the capital of Hungary. They lay a wreath on the statue of Petofi, a great hero who was one of his country's leaders when the people had risen in rebellion a century before. Then the crowds march off again shouting 'Ruszki, haza!' (Russians go home). Some shouted, 'Nagy to the Government. Rakosi into the Danube!'

Rakosi was Hungary's most hated man. One of Stalin's closest supporters, he had ruled Hungary since 1949. They had been bad years. Peasants had been forced into collective farms. The amount of food grown had fallen off greatly. Rakosi's men had bungled plans for new industries; steel works had been built where there was no iron or coal.

The Hungarian revolt. Budapest people decorate a huge head of Stalin with traffic signs. The head came from a statue which they had toppled over

The Hungarians were tired of paying for such costly mistakes.

But worse was Rakosi's cruelty. His secret police, the AVH, showed no mercy to any one who disagreed with him or Stalin. Peasants who objected to collective farms had been driven away from their homes. Many citizens had been forced to leave their homes in Budapest. It was well-known that the AVH used torture and Rakosi enjoyed watching them.

He had been so bad that very soon after Stalin's death he had been called to Moscow. One of the Russian leaders had angrily asked: 'Will you finally understand that you cannot govern forever with the support of Russian bayonets?' Because they thought he could not understand this, the Russians had sacked him as Prime Minister.

But now they wanted him to take over again. The Hungarian people were not having this. They broke out in revolt calling for Imre Nagy to lead the government. Nagy was the son of a peasant who had been in the government until he spoke out against collective farms. He was dismissed and only just escaped execution for Titoism.

The crowds grew more daring. Most of the Hungarian army went over to their side. The government called in Russian solders and tanks. The people attacked them with home made weapons. AVH men were seized and hanged. The government gave in. Rakosi fled and Nagy became Prime Minister.

An AVH man is hanged

23

Tanks in Budapest

Russian tanks in the centre of Budapest

Nagy wanted the Communist Party to stay in power and Hungary to stay friendly with the Russians. But he was forced to make changes by the anger of the Hungarian people. He got the Russians to take the Red Army away. He broke up the AVH. A new government was formed with men and women from other parties working alongside the communists. The Head of the Roman Catholic Church was freed from prison.

Away in Moscow, angry debates went on between the leaders of the Russian Communist Party. They had just given way to the Poles and some thought this had been weak. But Gomulka had kept the Communist Party firmly in charge. In Hungary, some Russians argued, Nagy was losing control. The Chinese Communists sent messages advising Russia to use force to stop the overthrow of a communist government. Then came the news that Nagy had said that Hungary was no longer a member of the Warsaw Pact, the arrangement which banded Russia and the satellites together for a possible war with the west. This was too much. Orders were given to invade.

On 4 November Nagy spoke on the radio:

'Today at dawn, Soviet troops launched an attack against the capital . . . Our troops are fighting. The government is at its post. I notify the people of our country and the entire world of these facts.'

Russian tanks rolled into Budapest, destroying whole streets to clear a few snipers. 27,000 Hungarians died. A quarter of a million fled abroad. Imre Nagy sheltered in the Yugoslav embassy. The Russians used a shabby trick to get him to leave. They arrested him and two years later hanged him.

The Hungarian revolution was crushed with great bloodshed but it was not a complete failure. No government since 1956 has dared to go back to the cruelty of Rakosi's day. Many people who were put in prison for their part in the revolution were set free. Writers have been allowed more freedom to say what they wish. Great care had been taken to make the lives of the people a little easier and gayer. Peasants were allowed to have their own small private farms while still working on collectives.

Russian shell fire damaged this building but Hungarians destroyed a tank and lorry

Czechoslovakia

Dear Comrade,

'I demand the heaviest penalty, the penalty of death for my father. Only now do I see that this creature . . . was my greatest and vilest enemy. Hatred towards my father will always strengthen me in my struggle for the communist future of our people.'

This was written in 1952 by a young man to the judge who was trying his father. The father was executed. Ten years later the Czechoslovak government announced that the evidence against him had been false. He had been a victim of Stalin's last purge.

This sad story shows how firm was Russian control over Czechoslovakia. The Czechs are an unlucky people; their land is the gateway to east Europe. Hitler seized it as the first step of his drive to the east. After 1945 the Russians wanted to be sure that it did not fall into unfriendly hands. They needed firm control because the Czechs are in some ways close to the people of western Europe. Their country has more modern industry than any other in east Europe. Until Hitler they had managed not to fall into the hands of a dictator like the rest of east Europe.

In the 1960s the Czechoslovak people began to turn against their pro-

Jan Masaryk, the Czech Foreign Minister, fell from his office window to his death in March 1948. He is thought to have killed himself to draw attention to the growing Communist control of Czechoslovakia

Mr Dubcek speaking to an audience in Czechoslovakia

Russian communist rulers. Many were ashamed of the shoddy goods in the shop windows of a country which once made high-quality articles. There were demands for free speech from teachers, writers and journalists. In January 1968 a quiet revolution began. The Czechoslovak Communist Party sacked their Stalinist leader Novotny. They gave his jobs to two men; Mr Dubcek who became Party leader and General Svoboda who was the country's new President.

Supporters of Novotny were dismissed. Industry was given more freedom to plan its own affairs. Freedom of speech returned. Discussions about politics took place on television, radio and in the newspapers.

This 'liberalisation' alarmed the Russians who feared that demands for the same freedom might come from the Russian people. In Bulgaria, Hungary and East Germany pro-Russian communist leaders thought that they might follow Novotny. Even Gomulka in Poland thought that freedom had gone too far. These countries were afraid that Dubcek's government might leave the Warsaw Pact; though there was really no sign that he would ever take this risk.

27

Czechoslovakia and the Russians

Russia and her friends in east Europe tried to stop the changes in Czechoslovakia. But Dubcek had the people behind him and prepared for even more changes in the communist system in Czechoslovakia.

They never took place. In August 1968 soldiers and tanks from Russia, Hungary, Bulgaria, East Germany and Poland entered Czechoslovakia. Paratroops landed in Prague, burst into Dubcek's office, handcuffed him and flew him to Moscow.

His life was saved by President Svoboda and the Czech People. Svoboda went to Moscow but refused to talk to the Russians until Dubcek and other captured Czech leaders joined him. At home the people stood up to the invaders. Radios broadcast from stations which the Russians never tracked down. Czechs surrounded Russian tanks and argued fiercely with young Russian soldiers who had been told

The end of a battle between Czech people and Russian tanks in Prague

they would be welcomed by the Czech people. The squares of Prague were packed with people listening to speakers protesting against the invasion.

The Czech parliament met and called for the Russians to leave. The Czech Communist Party elected Mr Dubcek as leader under the very noses of the invaders. The Russians tried to find a few Czechs who would take over from him. No-one came forward.

The Russians had to let Dubcek free and allow him to stay as leader of the Czechoslovak Communist Party. But they refused to move their tanks and troops out of Czechoslovakia until Dubcek had brought the country back to normal—normal from Russian point of view. This meant that, after he returned, he had to end the freedom he had given to the press and radio; once again everything had to be read by the censors before it appeared. Several important men in the government had to be dismissed because they had been responsible for pushing ahead with the most drastic changes. In 1969 Dubcek himself was dismissed.

President Svoboda

Divided Germany

Fear that Germany might again strike at the Soviet Union after passing through east Europe was strong in Stalin's mind in 1945. To prevent this eastern Europe was brought firmly into the Communist camp and Germany was divided. The division began in 1945 when Britain, America and France occupied the west and the Russians the east. In 1949 both sides set up German governments, the German Federal Republic in the west and the German Democratic Republic in the east. The issue of the two Germanys lay at the centre of the Cold War. The western nations did not recognise the GDR and the Communist states would not recognise the Federal Republic.

There was also conflict over Berlin. This capital of the old Germany lies in the GDR but half of it was occupied by the armies of the western powers. Berlin was not only a divided city; it was a gateway to the western world standing right in the Communist east.

In 1949 the GDR had 19 million people. There was little industry and the Communists forced German farmers to work long hours for low pay in hastily built factories. Most workers hated their new bosses. In 1953 revolts broke out which the GDR leaders could put down only with the help of Soviet troops. The east Germans found another way to show their dislike of Communism. By 1961, more than three million had

Life is better on both sides of the iron curtain but Europe is still divided. The pictures show American troops in a NATO exercise and soldiers of Communist nations in a Warsaw Pact exercise

fled to the west, most by simply passing from east to west Berlin. To stop them the East Germans built the Berlin Wall.

For ten more years no German leader in east or west would consider giving up the claim to rule the other half. Then Willy Brandt became West Germany's Chancellor and in December 1972 his government signed a treaty with East Germany. Each recognised the right of the other to rule in the lands it now holds. Willy Brandt went on to make a treaty with the Soviet Union and other Communist states. Most western powers recognised East Germany. Thus most of the world's states now agree that Germany should stay divided.

The Berlin Wall

To write

1 What are the capitals of Poland, Yugoslavia, Hungry and Czechoslovakia?
2 Write two or three sentences about each of these organisations: IMRO, the Comintern, the Chetniks, OZNA, the Warsaw Pact, the AVH.
3 What happened in Yugoslavian history on each of these dates: 1928, 1934, 1941, 1944, 1948, 1956
4 Make a list of the differences between the map of east Europe before the war (page 4) and the map of east Europe today (page 14).
5 Write two or three sentences about each of these men: Raditch, Gomulka, Nagy, Dubcek.
6 What did the governments of east Europe do to turn their countries into communist states?

For discussion

1 On page 10 it says, 'this was a cruel war in which both sides shot their prisoners!' What do you think of this?
2 Imagine you live in any of the east European countries. What would you think were the good and the bad sides of living under communist government?
3 Do you think east and west Germany should be re-united? Why or why not?
4 Do you think Titoism is a better form of government than Russian communism?
5 Give reasons for and against the Russian invasion of Hungary in 1956 and Czechoslovakia in 1968.

To find out

1 What has happened to Latvia, Estonia and Lithuania since the war?
2 Who is head of the government in East Germany, Poland and Czechoslovakia today?
3 Make a book of cuttings from newspapers on east Europe.
4 To which parts of eastern Europe do many people from Britain go on holiday? Why are these good holiday centres?
5 Which east European countries have a frontier which touches on Russia?
6 Through which countries does the river Danube flow. Name two large Polish rivers?